Date: 8/17/18

J 940.548673 KAL
Kallen, Stuart A.,
Navajo code talkers /

ALTERNATOR
BOOKS™

NAVAJO
CODE
TALKERS

Stuart A. Kallen

Lerner Publications ◆ Minneapolis

Publisher's note: The code developed by the Navajo was a closely guarded secret during World War II. Details of it weren't even recorded in military documents. Because of this secrecy, official military records about the code and its use in battle sometimes differ from the first-person accounts of Navajo code talkers. In those cases, we have chosen to use the facts as explained by the code talkers themselves, considering their words to be primary sources.

Content consultant: Judith Schiess Avila, coauthor of *Code Talker: The First and Only Memoir by One of the Original Navajo Code Talkers of WWII*

Lerner Publications Company
A division of Lerner Publishing Group, Inc.
241 First Avenue North
Minneapolis, MN 55401 USA

For reading levels and more information, look up this title at www.lernerbooks.com.

Library of Congress Cataloging-in-Publication Data

Names: Kallen, Stuart A., 1955– author.
Title: Navajo code talkers / Stuart A. Kallen.
Description: Minneapolis : Lerner Publications, 2018. | Series: Heroes of World War II | Includes bibliographical references and index.
Identifiers: LCCN 2017004839 (print) | LCCN 2017006215 (ebook) | ISBN 9781512486445 (library bound : alkaline paper) | ISBN 9781512498189 (eb pdf)
Subjects: LCSH: World War, 1939–1945—Cryptography—Juvenile literature. | Navajo code talkers—Juvenile literature. | Navajo Indians—History—20th century—Juvenile literature. | Navajo language—History—20th century—Juvenile literature. | World War, 1939–1945—Participation, Indian—Juvenile literature. | United States. Marine Corps—Indian troops—History—20th century—Juvenile literature.
Classification: LCC D810.C88 K35 2018 (print) | LCC D810.C88 (ebook) | DDC 940.54/8673—dc23

LC record available at https://lccn.loc.gov/2017004839

Manufactured in the United States of America
1-43468-33208-6/7/2017

CONTENTS

INTRODUCTION
STEADY GUNFIRE

In February 1945, a battle was raging on the South Pacific island of Iwo Jima. Bullets from a Japanese machine-gun nest rattled the air as bombs exploded. Navajo **code** talkers were part of a US Marine Corps **battalion** fighting the Japanese. As bullets whizzed

by their heads, the code talkers sent messages between troops on different parts of the island, such as "Need bulldozer on Green Beach immediately" and "Receiving steady machine gun and rifle fire."

Marine **commanders** got the messages and sent a bulldozer to Green Beach. The bulldozer knocked down barriers built by the enemy. A group of marines attacked the machine-gun nest. The enemy gunfire stopped, and dozens of US soldiers were saved.

US Marines take cover behind a hill at Iwo Jima in February 1945.

The US Marine Corps had invaded Iwo Jima on February 19, 1945. Six members of the Navajo Nation were part of the fighting force. The Navajo were there to **transmit** radio messages in a secret code based on their native language. During the next five weeks, the Navajo code talkers worked night and day under brutal combat conditions. They sent more than eight hundred messages about Japanese troop movements and enemy fire.

The fight on Iwo Jima was one of the most important battles of World War II (1939–1945). The United States had entered the war after hundreds of Japanese fighter planes attacked the US naval base at Pearl Harbor in

Marines land at Iwo Jima on February 19, 1945. About seventy-thousand US Marines and eighteen-thousand Japanese troops were involved in the battle.

Code talkers Henry Bake Jr. (*left*) and George H. Kirk in the jungle at the Battle of Bougainville in 1943

Hawaii on December 7, 1941. More than two thousand American soldiers and sailors were killed there. Some of the bloodiest battles between the United States and Japan took place on Pacific islands such as Iwo Jima, Peleliu, and Okinawa. Japanese forces had taken over such islands so they could launch attacks against American ships and planes. If the United States could build military bases there, it would be easier to fight nearby Japan. The Navajo code talkers and their secret code played a crucial role in every Pacific battle.

CHAPTER 1
A TALKING TRADITION

The Navajo people are a nation of American Indians. Most of their **reservation** is in northeastern Arizona and New Mexico. The US government forced the Navajo to move to this part of the country in 1864. The Navajo endured racism, poverty, and efforts to erase their traditional culture. Navajo people were not considered US citizens until 1924 and could not vote in Arizona until 1948.

Much of Navajo **culture** is based on oral storytelling. Before World War II, the Navajo language had never

Monument Valley Navajo Tribal Park, in Arizona and Utah, is part of the Navajo Nation, the reservation officially established in 1868.

The oral tradition of the Navajo applies to all important information. Even lists of things to remember are not written down.

been written down. The people did and still do memorize and tell one another everything they need to remember or to keep safe. Even the details of raising and selling sheep, an important trade for the Navajo, must be memorized and spoken.

Every Navajo child hears stories about the creation of the world. Parents and grandparents speak of animal spirits that look like eagles and coyotes. Children as young as three years old learn to repeat the stories word for word. As children grow older, the stories they learn get longer and more complex.

IDEAL LANGUAGE FOR A CODE

Telling and retelling stories prepared Navajo code
talkers for their role in World War II. Since Navajo
people were trained to memorize traditional stories,
they would be able to create and remember a code
that would eventually include more than seven
hundred words.

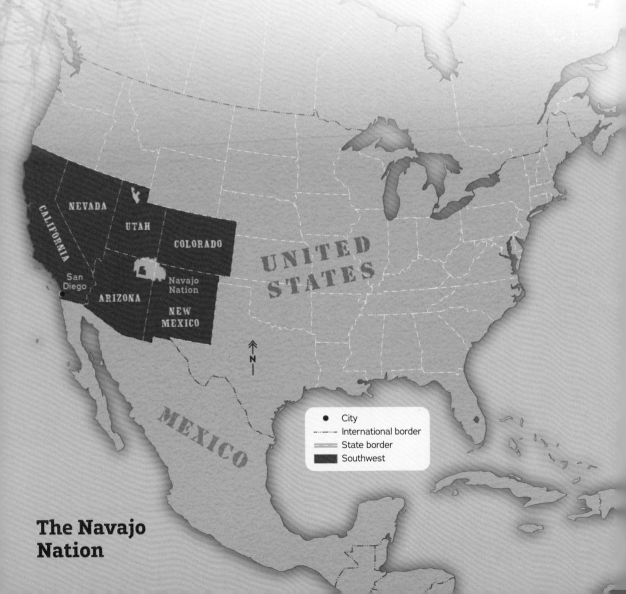

The Navajo Nation

The Navajo language was a perfect starting point for a secret code. The language had never been written down. Only thirty people who were not Navajo could speak the language. This meant that the enemy in Japan would never understand Navajo speakers. As Navajo code talker Chester Nez explained, "The language was not written, it could not be learned from a book. . . . [Saying] even one Navajo word is nearly impossible for someone not used to hearing the sounds that make up the language."

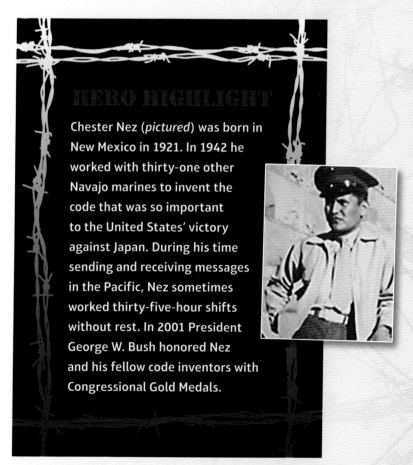

HERO HIGHLIGHT

Chester Nez (*pictured*) was born in New Mexico in 1921. In 1942 he worked with thirty-one other Navajo marines to invent the code that was so important to the United States' victory against Japan. During his time sending and receiving messages in the Pacific, Nez sometimes worked thirty-five-hour shifts without rest. In 2001 President George W. Bush honored Nez and his fellow code inventors with Congressional Gold Medals.

The Choctaw code talkers from World War I (*above*) inspired Philip Johnston to suggest that Navajo people might do something similar.

JOINING THE MARINES

Philip Johnston had grown up on the Navajo reservation in Arizona. He was not Navajo. Johnston's parents were religious **missionaries** who worked among the Navajo people. Johnston was a **veteran** of World War I (1914–1918). During that war, he heard about the success of Choctaw Indian code talkers. Choctaw soldiers had successfully used the Choctaw language to send coded messages during battle.

In 1942 Johnston suggested that the Navajo could perform the same service for the Marine Corps. He set up a demonstration for several Marine Corps officers. The Navajo showed how they might send coded messages in their native language. The officers were impressed with the results. The Marine Corps recruited twenty-nine Navajo men for a top-secret, potentially dangerous project. The young men didn't know it yet, but they would soon create and use a secret code that was impossible for the enemy to understand.

A group of the original twenty-nine Navajo recruits

CHAPTER 2
CREATING CODES

In April 1942, the Navajo recruits were sent to San
Diego, California, where they trained as marines. After
completing basic training, they were told their secret
mission: inventing a code. The Navajo then spent
months working to create and learn a complex code
in their native language. Each letter of the English
alphabet was given an English code word starting

**Navajo marines take a break from
basic training at Camp Elliott in
San Diego in 1942.**

with that letter, such as the names of common animals, plants, and objects. The English code words were then **translated** into Navajo. The letter *A* became ant, then *wol-la-chee* in Navajo. *B* became bear, or *shush* in the Navajo language. This system allowed the Navajo speakers to spell out English words in a code the enemy would never understand.

The Navajo also invented code words for common military objects. The Navajo word for hummingbird was used to describe a fighter plane. A battleship was a whale, a hand grenade was a potato, and a bomb was an egg. The Navajo soldiers memorized hundreds of

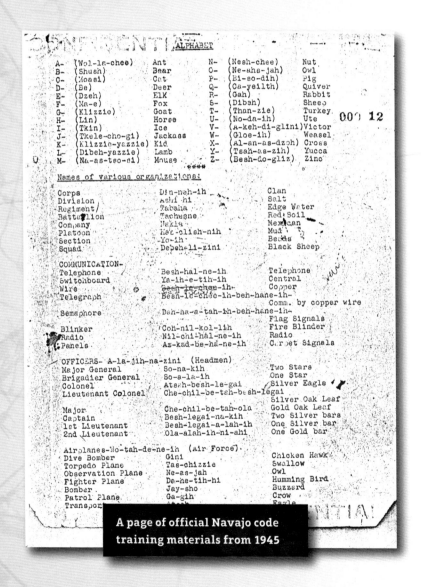

A page of official Navajo code training materials from 1945

these terms. They would need to use their code on the battlefield without error. Thousands of marines were depending on them.

The Navajo code was meant to replace a code-making machine called the M-209. The military used the M-209 to create the code, send it, and decode messages after they were received. The Marine Corps tested several Navajo speakers to see if they could match the speed of the M-209. The M-209 took thirty minutes to create and send a code. The Navajo soldiers did it in only twenty seconds.

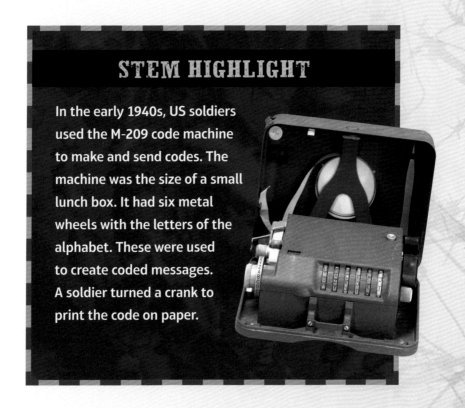

STEM HIGHLIGHT

In the early 1940s, US soldiers used the M-209 code machine to make and send codes. The machine was the size of a small lunch box. It had six metal wheels with the letters of the alphabet. These were used to create coded messages. A soldier turned a crank to print the code on paper.

CHAPTER 3
INTO BATTLE

In August 1942, thousands of marines invaded the island of Guadalcanal to fight the Japanese. Japan had taken control of Guadalcanal, along with several other islands in the South Pacific, in the months after the Pearl Harbor bombing.

Three code talkers work through a problem during Marine Corps training. From left to right: Peter Nahaidinae, Joe Gatewood, and Lloyd Oliver.

The marines were able to gain a foothold on Guadalcanal and build a military base. US soldiers used the base to launch attacks on Japanese forces that controlled the small island. Thousands of soldiers on both sides were killed in battle.

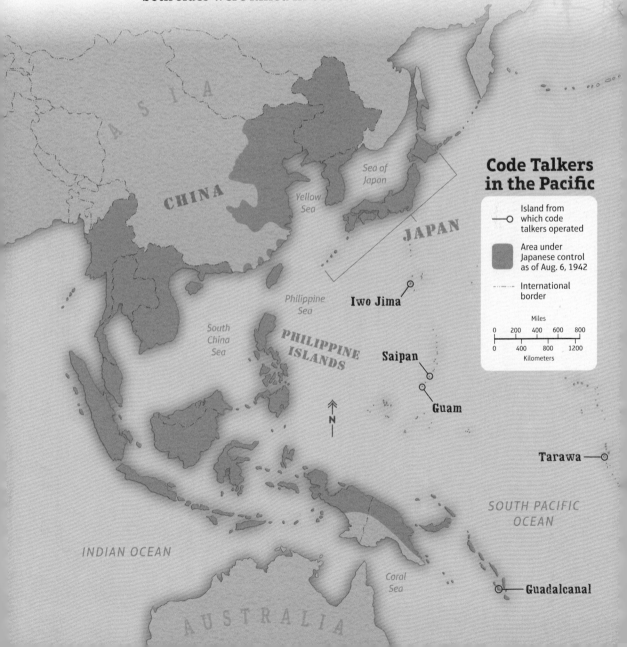

Code Talkers in the Pacific

—○ Island from which code talkers operated

■ Area under Japanese control as of Aug. 6, 1942

----- International border

Miles
0   200   400   600   800

0   400   800   1200
Kilometers

"DESTROY"

In November 1942, the Navajo code talkers arrived on Guadalcanal for their first mission. The Navajo soldiers worked around the clock in teams of two. They set up communications outposts with two-way radios known as SCR-300s. The code talkers received messages written in English from Marine Corps commanders. The Navajo mentally translated the messages into code. Then they repeated the messages into the radio to a code talker on the other end.

STEM HIGHLIGHT

The Navajo code talkers sent and received messages using a two-way, battery-operated radio, the SCR-300. Users spoke into an old-style telephone receiver. Soldiers carried the 35-pound (16 kg) radio in a large backpack (*pictured*). Since users could walk and talk while using the SCR-300, soldiers nicknamed the radio a walkie-talkie.

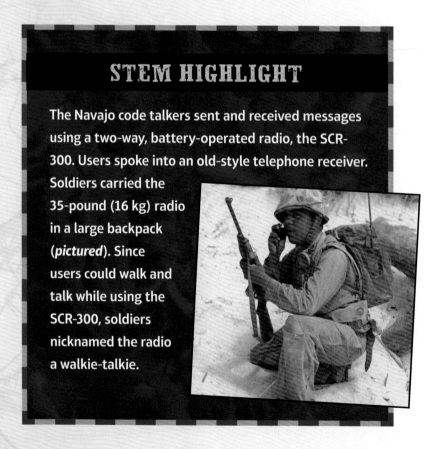

Nez recalled the first coded message he sent from the battlefield: "Enemy machine-gun nest on your right flank. Destroy." (In Navajo: *"Beh-na-ali-tsosie a-knah-as-donih ah-toh nish-na-jih-goh dah-di-kad ah-deel-tahi."*) Another team received his message. US **artillery** destroyed the Japanese gun nest within minutes.

Marine corporal Lloyd Oliver served as a Navajo code talker, a sniper, and a scout during the war.

SEEING ACTION

With the help of the code talkers, the marines defeated the Japanese on Guadalcanal in February 1943. After this success, the Marine Corps recruited more Navajo and trained them to speak the code. By the end of the war in 1945, more than four hundred code talkers had served in some of the fiercest battles of World War II. No one was ever able to crack the code created by the Navajo code talkers, a rare feat for a code used in battle.

Code talkers and cousins Preston Toledo (*left*) and Frank Toledo send messages over a radio in the South Pacific in July 1943.

US Marines put up an American flag at Iwo Jima in February 1945 after taking a key Japanese fortress.

During the first two days of the Iwo Jima invasion in February 1945, the code talkers worked for twenty-four hours straight. They sent and decoded more than eight hundred messages without error. In every battle, the heroic deeds of the code talkers gave the US forces an edge.

In March 1945, the Marine Corps achieved victory at Iwo Jima. As Major Howard Connor said after the fight, "Were it not for the Navajos, the Marines would never have taken Iwo Jima."

CHAPTER 4
HONORING THE CODE TALKERS

World War II ended when Japan surrendered on August 14, 1945. The cost of victory was high. More than 111,000 American soldiers had been killed in action. Among the dead were thirteen Navajo code talkers.

Many of the code talkers received medals for acts of heroism. But after the war, the Navajo soldiers were not allowed to tell anyone about the lifesaving code they had created. The military wanted to keep the code

The 382nd platoon was made up of the Navajo marines who created the secret code used in the war.

382nd PLATOON U.S.M.C. SAN DIEGO
1942
US MARINES — FIRST TO FIGHT

secret, in case it was needed again. Nez was told by his commanders: "When you get home . . . don't tell your people, your parents, family, don't tell them what your job was. . . . Don't talk about it."

The code talkers kept their role in the war secret for more than twenty years. Then, in 1968, the government **declassified** the code talker program. That meant it was no longer secret and the Navajo could tell their stories. In 1971 sixty-nine World War II veterans formed the Navajo Code Talkers Association. The group marched in parades, visited schools, and talked about their role in the war on radio and TV shows.

Navajo code talker John Brown Jr. (*right*) and President George W. Bush at a Congressional Gold Medal ceremony in 2001

THEY DEFEATED THE ENEMY

In 1982 President Ronald Reagan named August 14 National Navajo Code Talkers Day. Reagan called upon the nation to join in a tribute to the Navajo war heroes. In 2001 the code talkers were awarded medals for their special service. The original twenty-nine were given Congressional Gold Medals. A message on the back stated, "With the Navajo language they defeated the enemy."

The Navajo code talkers became role models for young American Indians—and for people everywhere. As code talker Samuel Tso explained, "I was fighting for all the Indian people. All the people in the United States, all that we had."

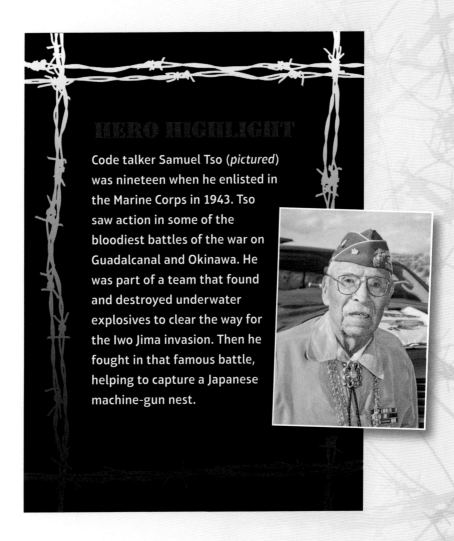

HERO HIGHLIGHT

Code talker Samuel Tso (*pictured*) was nineteen when he enlisted in the Marine Corps in 1943. Tso saw action in some of the bloodiest battles of the war on Guadalcanal and Okinawa. He was part of a team that found and destroyed underwater explosives to clear the way for the Iwo Jima invasion. Then he fought in that famous battle, helping to capture a Japanese machine-gun nest.

TIMELINE

December 7, 1941	Japanese military forces bomb Pearl Harbor, an American naval base in Hawaii.
February 1942	The Marine Corps tests Philip Johnston's idea of using the Navajo language for a military code.
April and May 1942	The US Marines recruit twenty-nine Navajo to invent a code in their native language.
September 1942	The first Navajo code talkers go into battle on Guadalcanal.
1942–1945	Navajo code talkers fight in every Marine Corps assault in the Pacific region.
August 14, 1945	Japan surrenders, ending World War II. Navajo code talkers are sworn to secrecy and told to never mention their role in war.

1968	The US government declassifies information about the Navajo code talkers.
1971	Navajo veterans form the Code Talkers Association to educate the public about the role of the code talkers in the war.
1982	President Reagan names August 14 National Navajo Code Talkers Day.
2001	President George W. Bush presents Congressional Gold Medals to the original twenty-nine code talkers.
2014	Chester Nez, the last of the original Navajo who developed the code, dies at the age of ninety-three.

Source Notes

5 Sally McClain, *Navajo Weapon* (Boulder, CO: Books Beyond Borders, 1994), 168.

11 Chester Nez and Judith Schiess Avila, *Code Talker* (New York: Berkley Caliber, 2011), 91.

21 Ibid. 133.

23 Alex Molnar Jr., "Navajo Code Talkers: World War II History & Facts," California Indian Education, August 1997, http://www.californiaindianeducation.org/native_american_veterans/navajo_code_talkers.html.

25 "Recognition," National Museum of the American Indian, accessed February 15, 2017, http://www.nmai.si.edu/education/codetalkers/html/chapter7.html.

26 Ibid.

27 Ibid.

Glossary

artillery: large guns used in war

battalion: a large unit of soldiers

code: a system of words, letters, or symbols used to send secret messages

commanders: people in charge of soldiers or military operations

culture: the arts, customs, and traditions of a group of people

declassified: formerly secret information made public

missionaries: people working to spread their religious beliefs

reservation: a piece of land the government sets aside for a specific purpose

translated: words changed from one language to another language

transmit: to pass something from one place to another

veteran: a person who served in the military

FURTHER INFORMATION

Lowery, Linda. *Native Peoples of the Southwest*. Minneapolis: Lerner Publications, 2017.

Native Words, Native Warriors
http://www.nmai.si.edu/education/codetalkers/html/index.html

Navajo Code: Interviews
http://navajocodetalkers.org/category/interviews/

"Navajo Code Talkers and the Unbreakable Code"
https://www.cia.gov/news-information/featured-story
-archive/2008-featured-story-archive/navajo-code-talkers/

"Navajo Code Talkers History"
http://navajopeople.org/navajo-code-talker.htm

Owens, Lisa L. *Attack on Pearl Harbor*. Minneapolis: Lerner Publications, 2018.

Rickard, Kris A., and Raymond Bial. *The People and Culture of the Navajo*. New York: Cavendish Square, 2016.

Index

Photo Acknowledgments

The images in this book are used with the permission of: © iStockphoto. com/akinshin (barbed wire backgrounds throughout); © iStockphoto. com/ElementalImaging (camouflage background throughout); Mondadori Portfolio/Newscom, p. 4–5; akg-images/Newscom, p. 6; National Archives, pp. 7, 29; Library of Congress, Carol M. Highsmith Archive (LC-DIG-highsm-16379), p. 8; Library of Congress, Pennington & Rowland, C. C. (ca. 1914) Relating an Experience (LC-USZ62-99571), p. 9; © Laura Westlund/ Independent Picture Service, pp. 10, 19; ZUMA Press Inc/Alamy Stock Photo, pp. 11, 13; © iStockphoto.com/aaron007, pp. 11, 27 (barbed wire frame); RODGER MALLISON/MCT/Newscom, p. 12; Official USMC Photograph, provided by the Command Museum, MCRD, San Diego, pp. 14, 18, 20, 22, 24, 28, 29; Northern Arizona University, Cline Library (Johnston, Philip), p. 15; Northern Arizona University, Cline Library (Navajo Code Talkers), p. 16; © Rama/Wikimedia Commons (CC BY-SA 2.0 FR), p. 17; Everett Collection Inc/ Alamy Stock Photo, p. 21; Pictorial Press Ltd/Alamy Stock Photo, p. 23; Hemis/ Alamy Stock Photo, p. 25; REUTERS/Alamy Stock Photo, p. 26; Charles Mann/ Alamy Stock Photo, p. 27.

Front cover: © Corbis/Getty Images (main); © iStockphoto.com/akinshin (barbed wire background); © iStockphoto.com/ElementalImaging (camouflage background); © iStockphoto.com/MillefloreImages (flag background).